LUNCH TIME

I couldn't find
my lunch today.

I was hungry!

3

"I have some sandwiches,"
said Peter.

4

So he shared his
sandwiches with me.

"I have some raisins,"
said Matt.

So he shared
his raisins with me.

"I have some fruit,"
said Sue.

So she shared
her fruit with me.

"I have some crackers," said Erica.

So she shared
her crackers with me.

"Look, Lara,"
said my teacher.

"I've found your lunch."

I wasn't hungry
anymore.

So I shared my lunch
with my friends!